A QUICK LOOK AT ASIA
THE WORLD'S MOST POPULOUS CONTINENT

Geography Grade 3
Children's Geography & Cultures Books

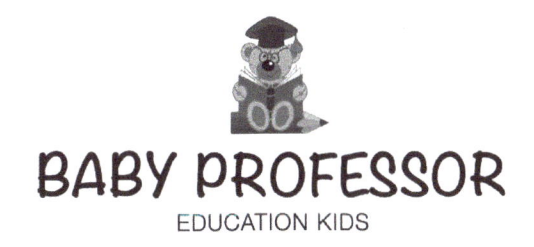

BABY PROFESSOR
EDUCATION KIDS

Speedy Publishing LLC
40 E. Main St. #1156
Newark, DE 19711
www.speedypublishing.com
Copyright 2017

All Rights reserved. No part of this book may be reproduced or used in any way or form or by any means whether electronic or mechanical, this means that you cannot record or photocopy any material ideas or tips that are provided in this book

In this book, we're going to cover an introduction to the Asian continent's geography and highlights from some of its many countries. So let's get right to it!

THE CONTINENT OF ASIA

Asia is Earth's largest continent in terms of landmass and also in terms of population. Over 60% of the world's population, over 4.4 billion people live there. Of that 4.4 billion, approximately 1.4 billion live in China. Even though Asia has so many people, about two-thirds of its landmass is too cold or dry to be comfortably inhabited.

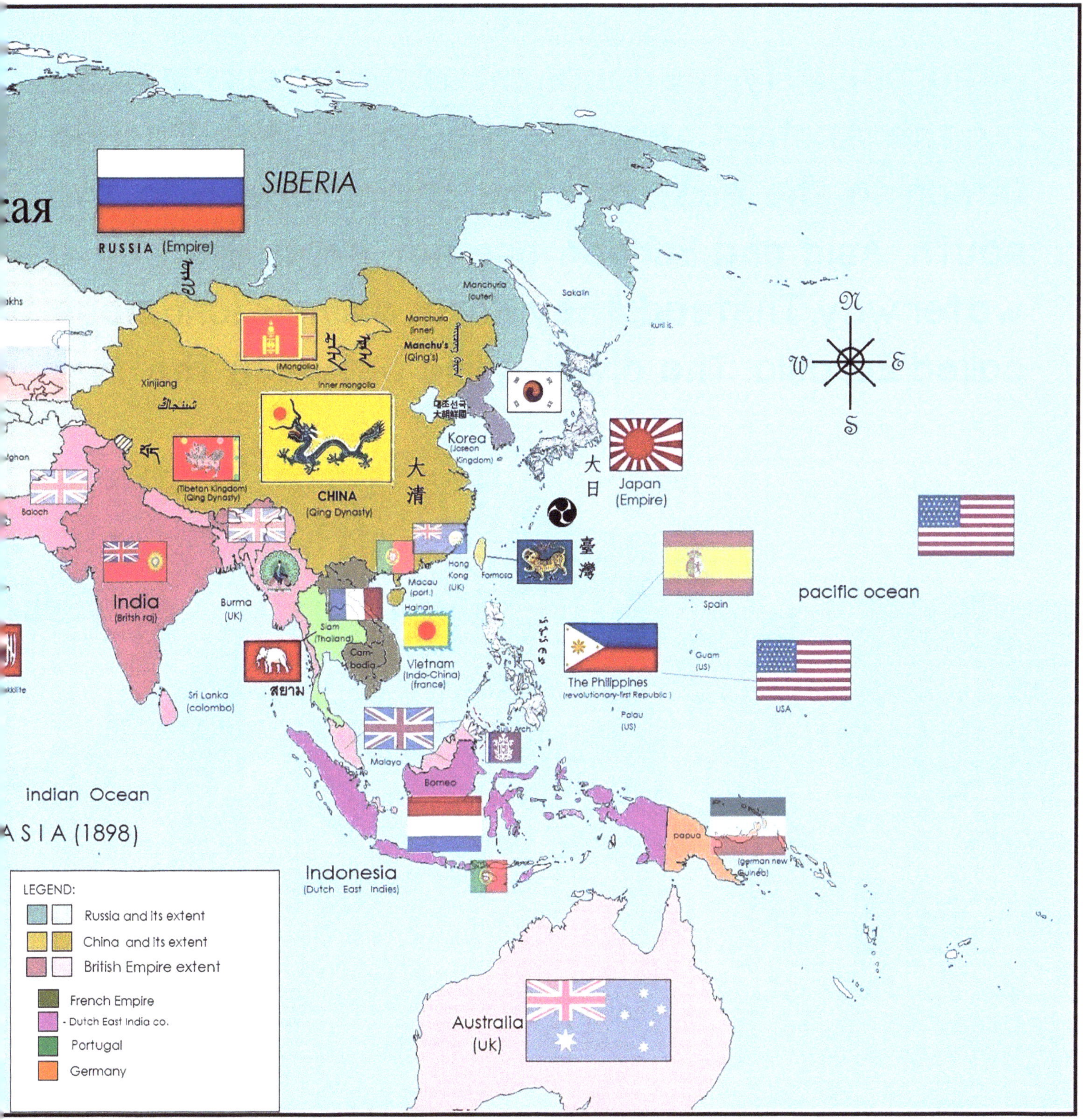
SIBERIA
RUSSIA (Empire)
Manchuria (outer)
Sakalin
kuril is.
Manchuria (inner)
Manchu's (Qing's)
(Mongolia)
Inner mongolia
Xinjiang
(Tibetan Kingdom) (Qing Dynasty)
CHINA (Qing Dynasty)
大清
Korea (Joseon Kingdom)
大日
Japan (Empire)
Baloch
India (Britsh raj)
Burma (UK)
Macau (port.)
Hong Kong (UK)
Formosa
臺灣
Hainan
Siam (Thailand)
สยาม
Cam-bodia
Vietnam (Indo-China) (france)
Spain
pacific ocean
The Philippines (revolutionary-first Republic)
Guam (US)
USA
Palau (US)
Sri Lanka (colombo)
Sulu Arch.
Malaya
Borneo
papua
(german new Guinea)
indian Ocean
ASIA (1898)
Indonesia (Dutch East Indies)
Australia (uk)
LEGEND:
Russia and its extent
China and its extent
British Empire extent
French Empire
- Dutch East India co.
Portugal
Germany

Geographically, the continent of Asia is surrounded by the Arctic Ocean to the north, the Pacific Ocean to the east, and the Indian Ocean to the south. Asia and Europe are not separated by a waterway. Instead, they form a single landmass called Eurasia. The dividing line between the two continents of Europe and Asia is considered to be the Ural Mountains, the Ural River to the Caspian Sea, and the Caucasus Mountains. Asia connects with Africa at the Isthmus of Suez. North America is within 60 miles (97 kilometers) of Asia at the location of the Bering Strait.

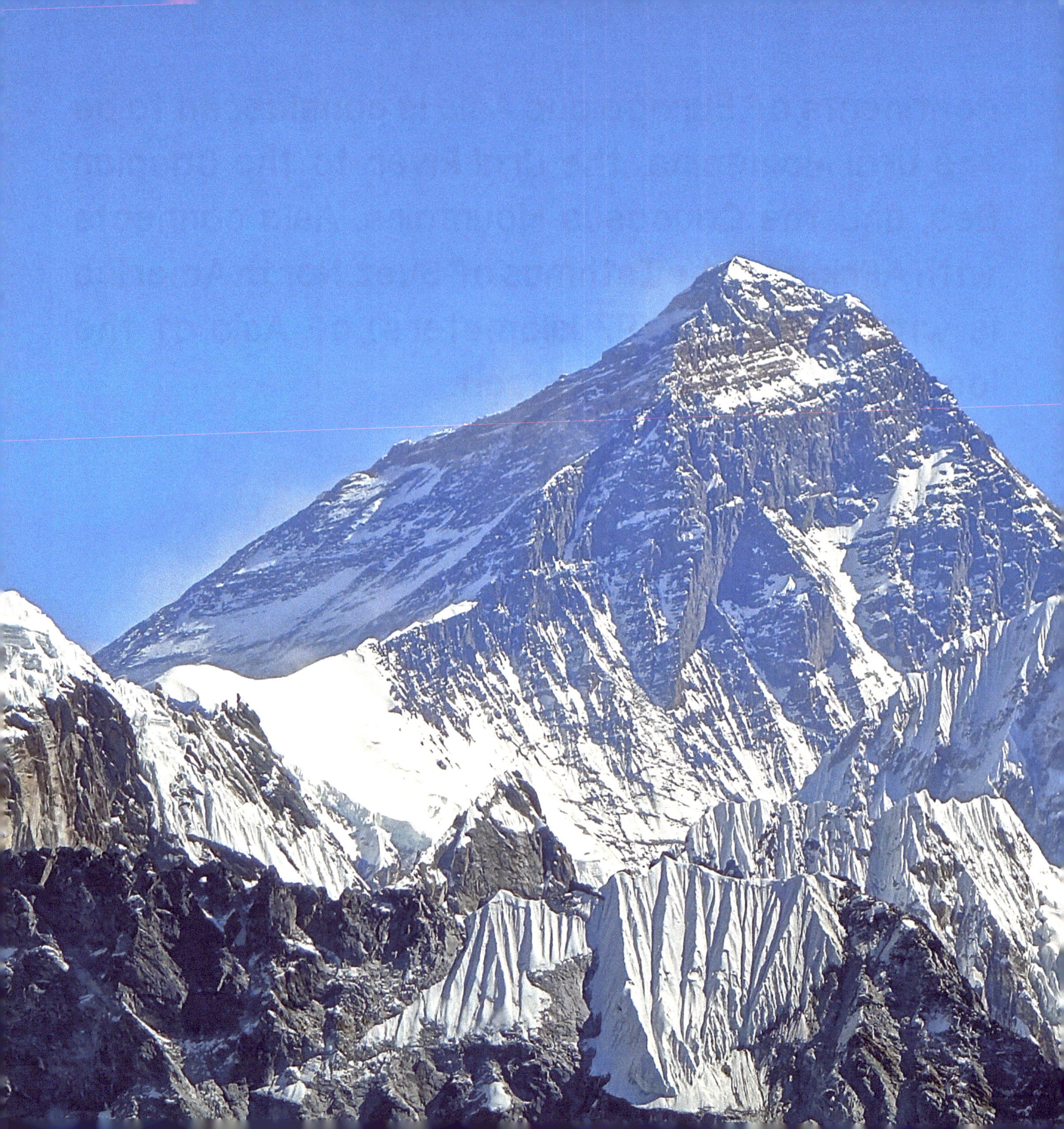

GEOGRAPHICAL FEATURES OF THE CONTINENT

The continent of Asia has a land area of 17.2 million square miles or 44.5 million square kilometers. It covers about 30% of all Earth's land. The highest mountain peak is Mount Everest, which is located in Nepal. It is over 29,000 feet or 8,848 meters tall. The largest salt lake is the Caspian Sea. It covers 143,250 square miles or 371,000 square kilometers. The continent's longest river is the Yangtze River in China. It is 3,964 miles long or 6,380 kilometers.

HIGHLIGHTS OF SOME OF ASIA'S FASCINATING COUNTRIES

There are over 40 countries located in Asia. The world's two most populated countries, China and India, are in Asia. Asia is so large that it is divided into different regions.

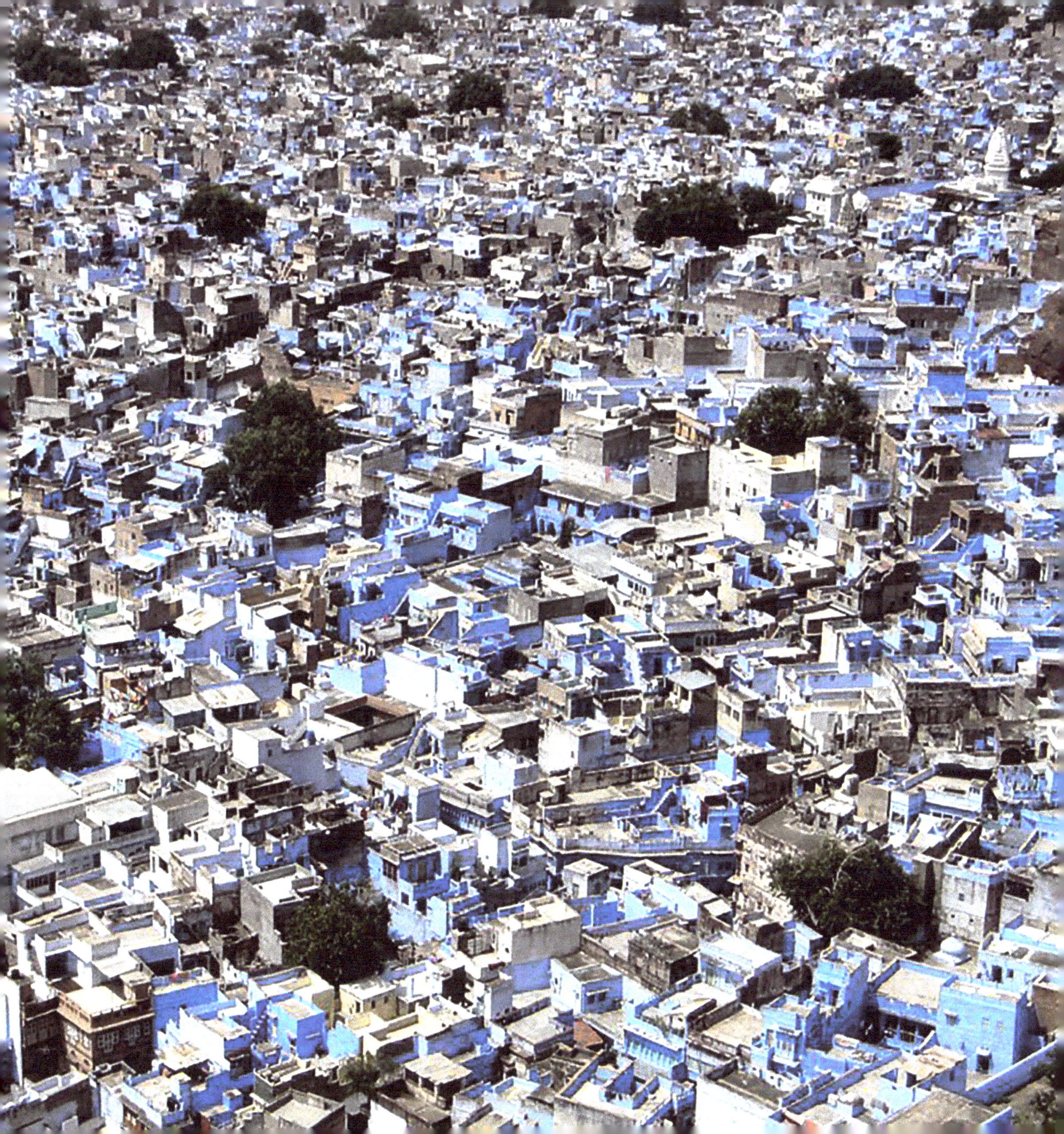

SOUTH ASIA

INDIA

The Taj Mahal is a white marble building that is a symbol of India. The construction of the building started in 1631. It took 22 years to build with a staff of 20,000 workers. Thirty different varieties of precious stones were used to beautify the building. Its architecture is a combination of Islamic, Persian, and Indian styles.

NEPAL

Landlocked between India and China, Nepal is known for its mountain peaks. It contains eight of the ten highest peaks in the world including Mount Everest, which is the tallest. It also contains Kanchenjunga, which is the third tallest.

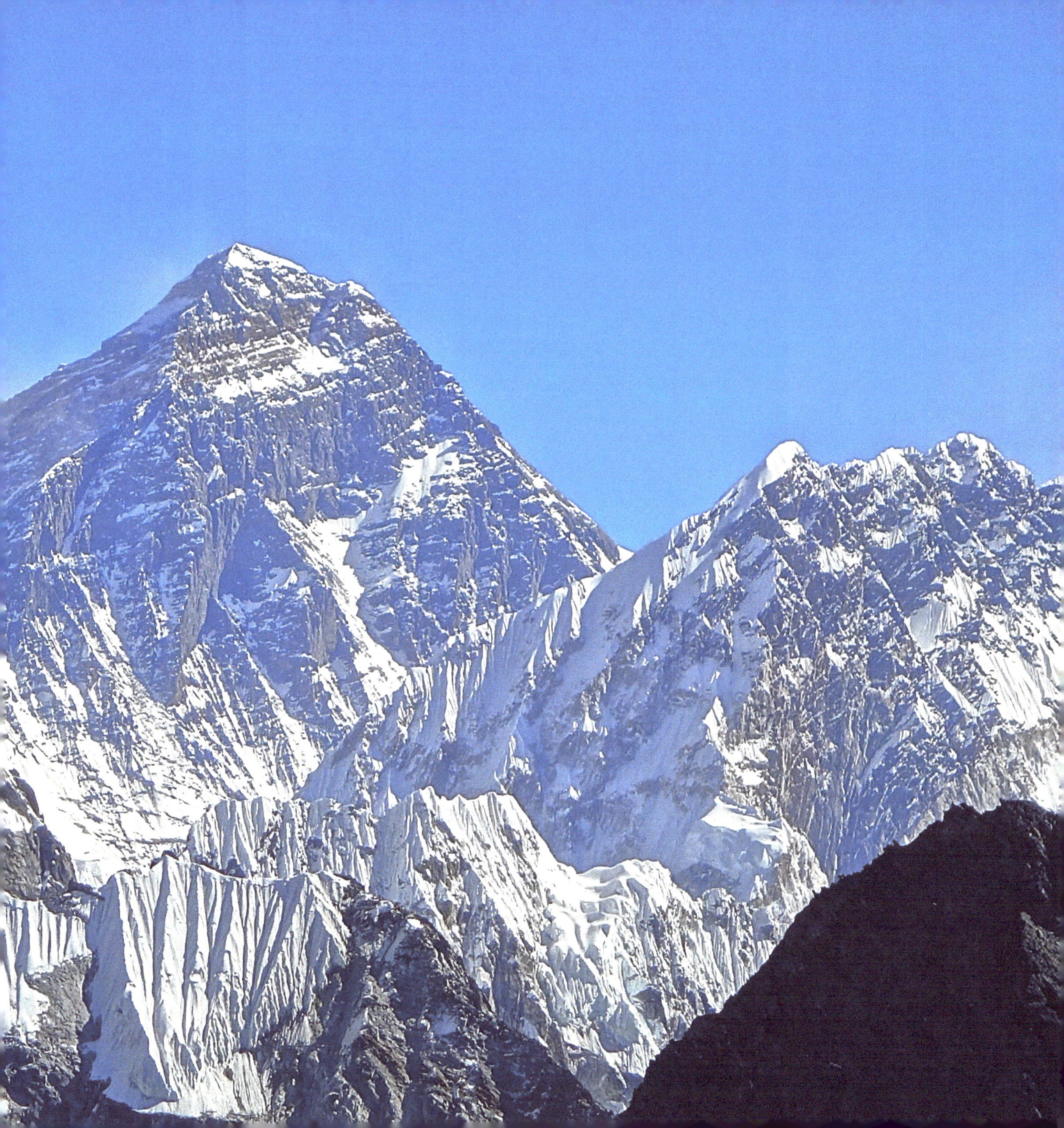

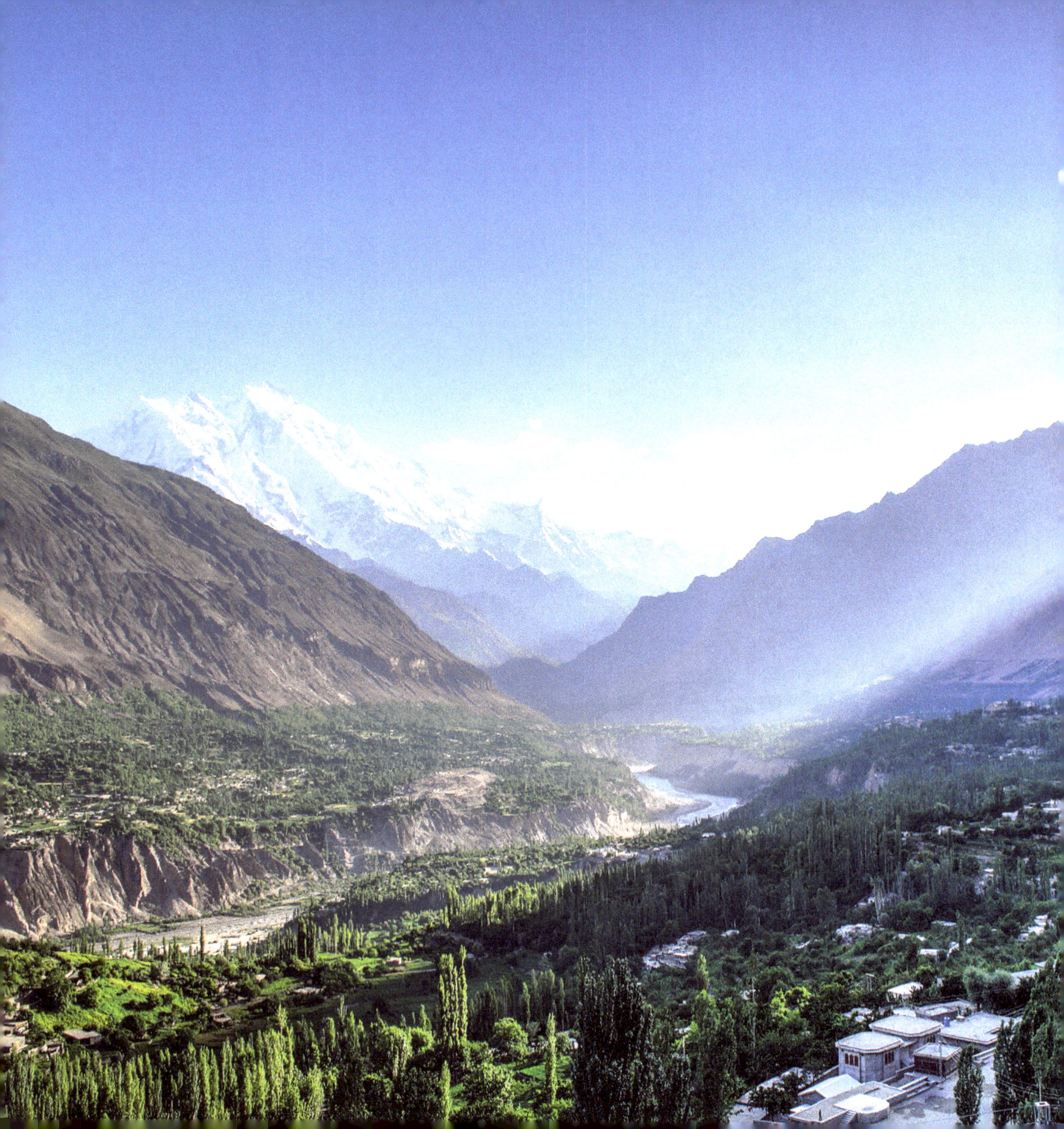

PAKISTAN

The Hunza Valley, a region in northernmost Pakistan, is famous for its natural scenery of beautiful mountains and shimmering lakes. It's also known for its long-lived people.

CAMBODIA

During the monsoon season, the Tonle Sap Lake in Cambodia swells to one of the largest freshwater lakes in Asia. People live in nomadic floating villages near the shoreline. There are 100 varieties of water birds as well as crocodiles and turtles in this habitat.

SOUTHEAST ASIA

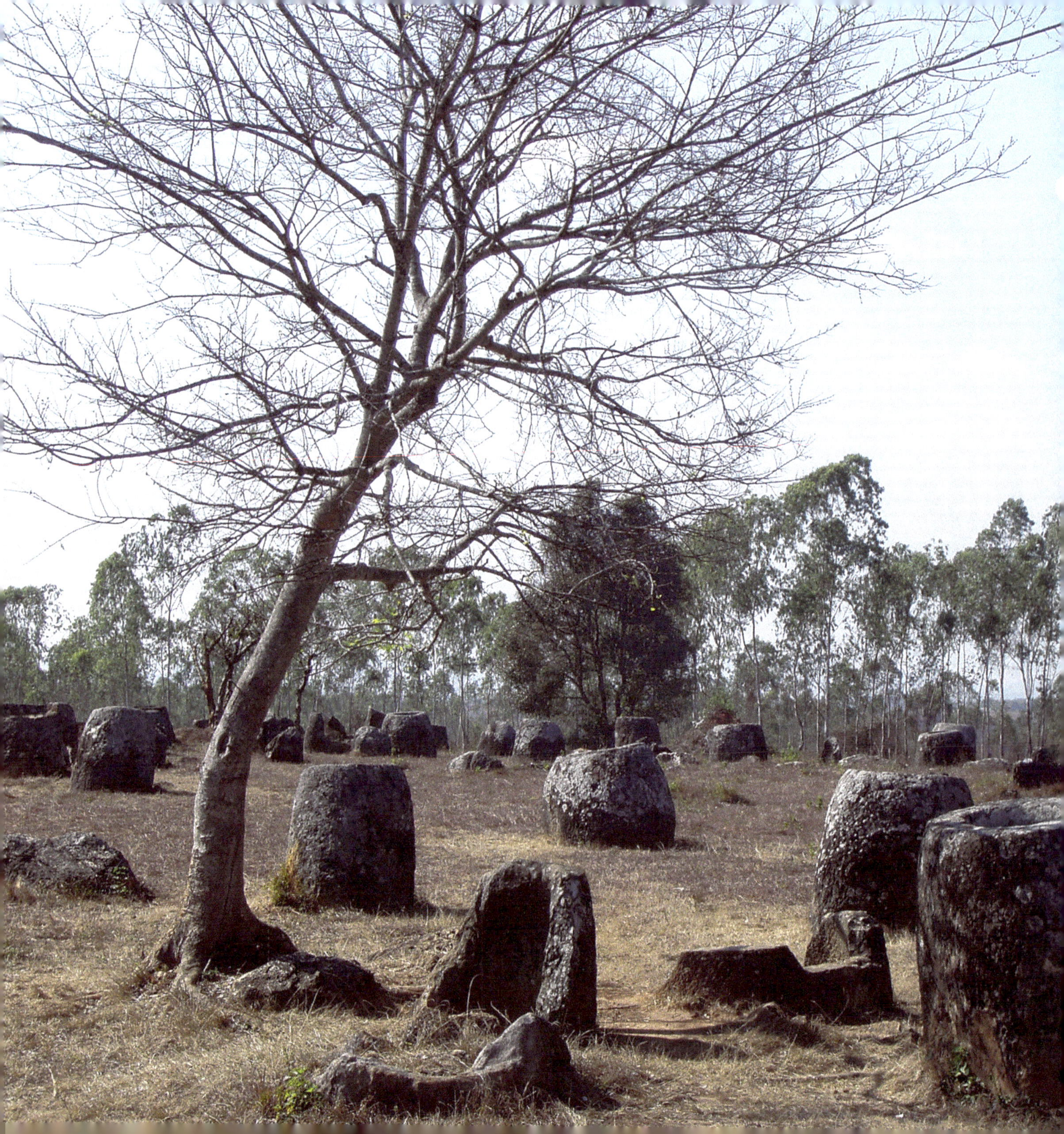

LAOS

In the country of Laos there is a mysterious area of the Xieng Khouang plateau called the c. Scattered there are thousands of megalithic stone jars about 2,000 years old. The tallest stone jars are nearly 10 feet high. No one knows exactly who made the jars or what their purpose was.

MYANMAR

The country of Myanmar, formerly called Burma, has a population consisting of more than 100 different ethnic groups. One of its most famous landmarks is the gold-plated Shwedagon Pagoda containing many Buddhist relics that date back to the 6th century.

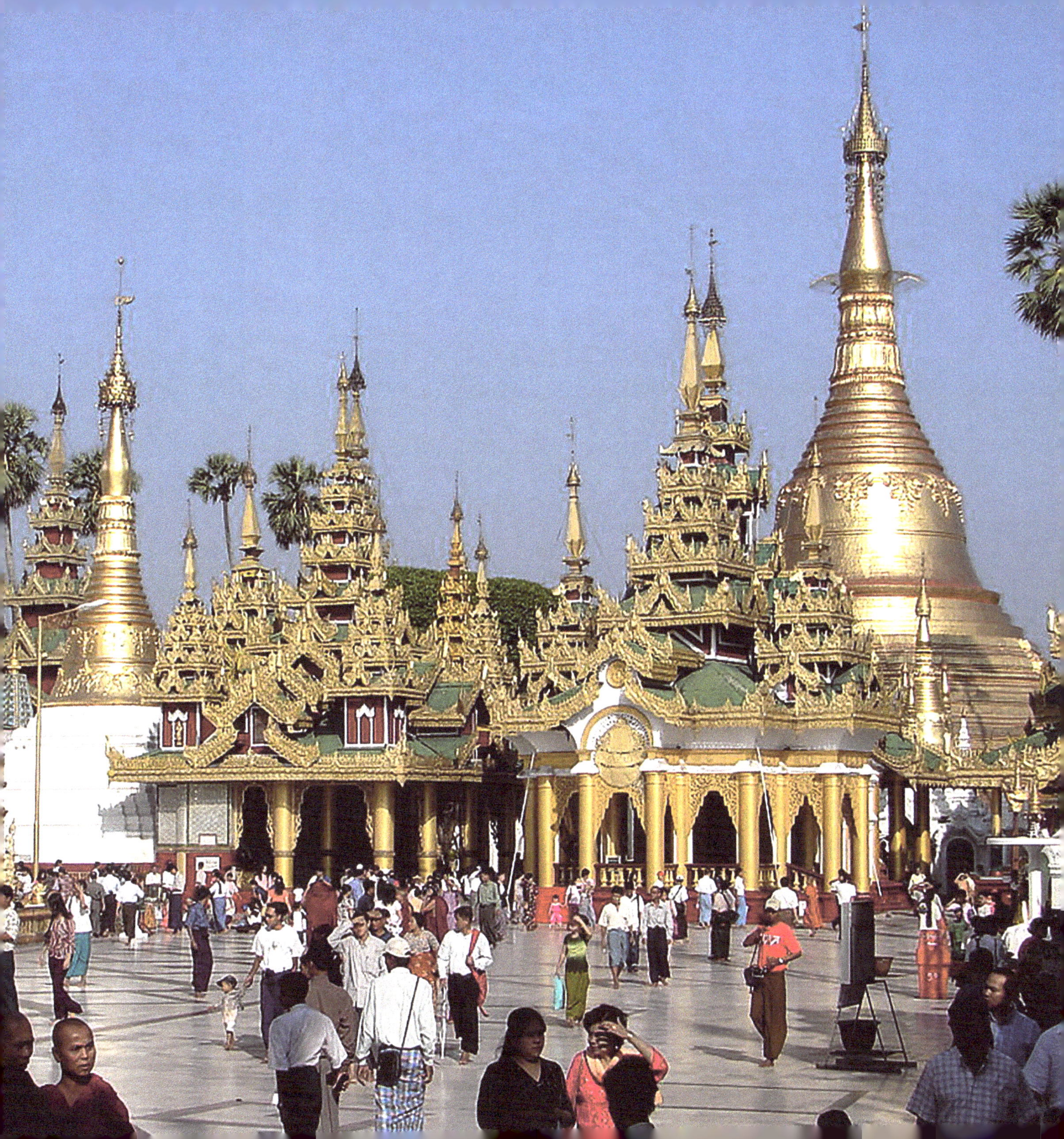

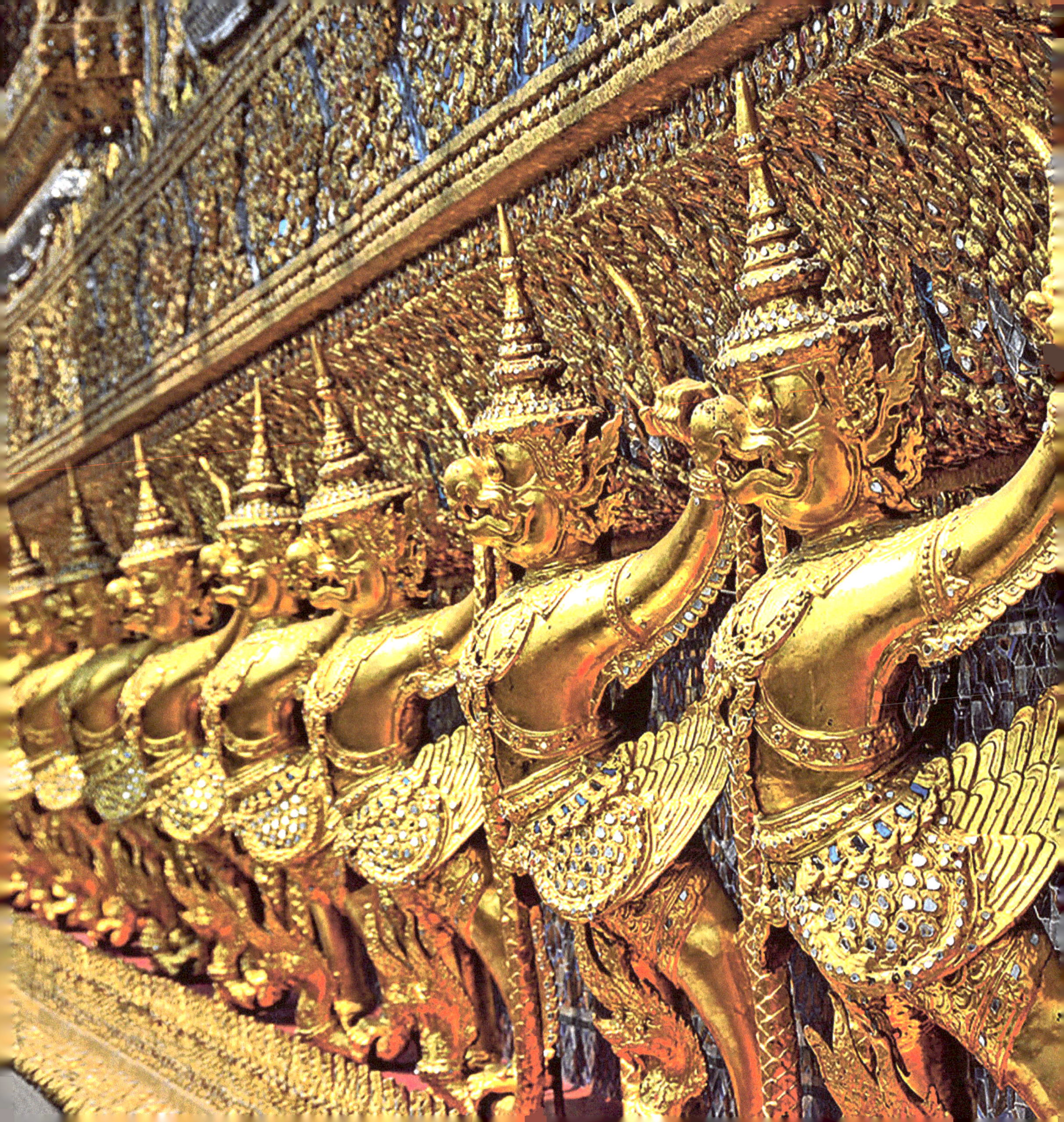

THAILAND

One of the most amazing places in Thailand is the Temple of the Emerald Buddha in Bangkok. Inside the temple, is Thailand's most sacred shrine, the Bot, which means "house of meditation." Within the Bot is the sacred 500-year-old, 26-inch high Emerald Buddha.

VIETNAM

The country of Vietnam has a long coastline along the South China Sea. The Red River in the north and the Mekong River in the south spread over its swampy delta plains. These plains are the perfect type of ground for crops such as rice.

INDONESIA

Komodo National Park is located within the volcanic islands called Lesser Sunda in Indonesia. This is the only place in the world the giant lizards called "Komodo dragons" live. They grow to an average of 6.5-9.8 feet long.

MALAYSIA

The country of Malaysia is made up of two main landmasses that are separated by the South China Sea. It shares borders with Indonesia, Thailand, and Brunei. It's also linked to Singapore by a causeway and bridge. A famous landmark in Kuala Lumpur, Malaysia consists of the 88-story Petronas Twin Towers. There is a skybridge that connects the two towers and offers visitors a breathtaking view of the city from 42 stories up.

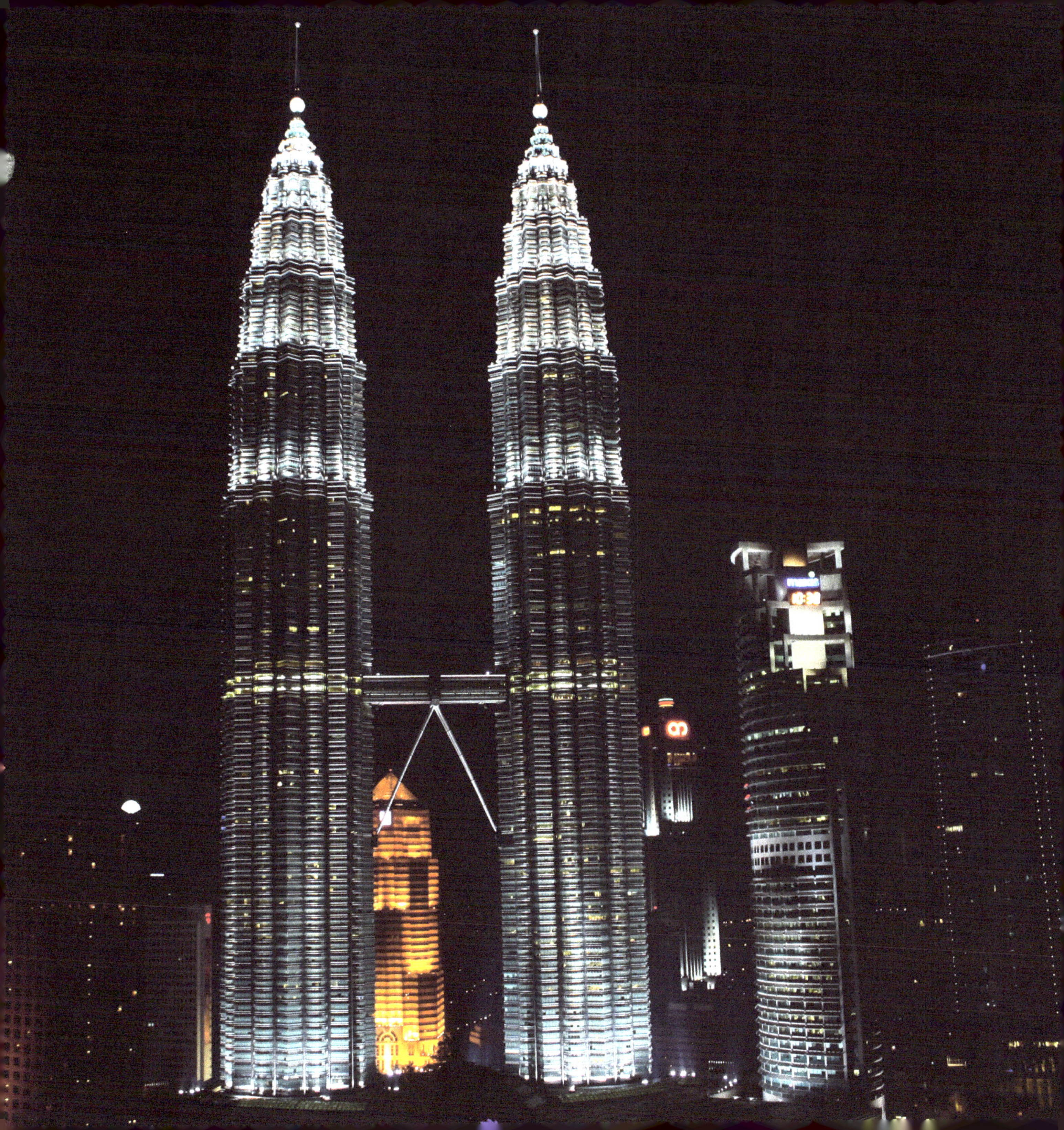

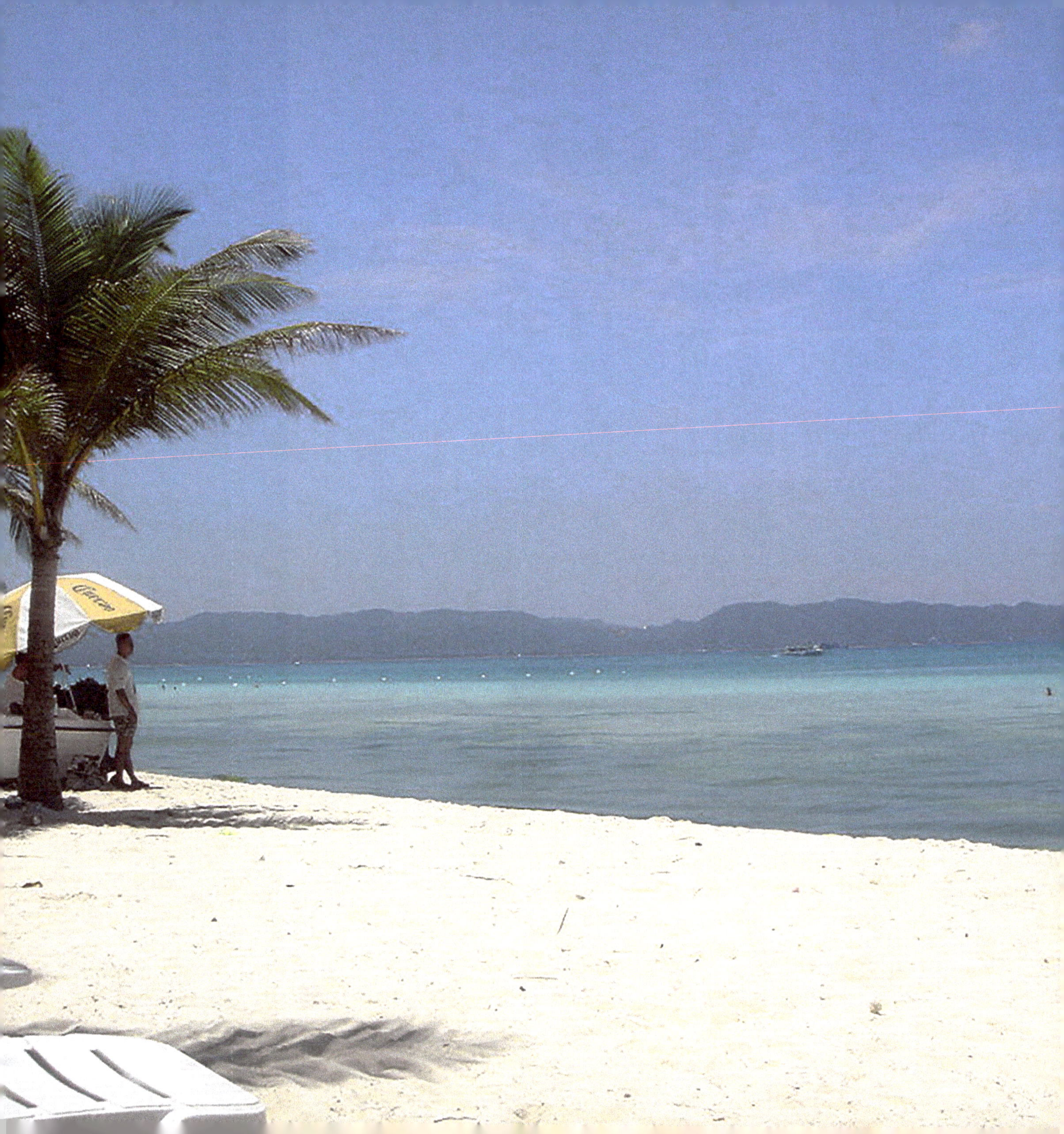

PHILIPPINES

The country of the Philippines is made up of over 7,000 islands. Its capital city of Manila is known for its waterfront highway, Roxas Boulevard, which is lined with coconut trees and runs along the shores of Manila Bay. It's also known for its white sand beaches.

MACAU

A small peninsula in China, Macau belonged to Portugal until 1999 and has its own economic and legal system. It's known for its huge malls and giant casinos, giving it the nickname of "the Las Vegas of Asia."

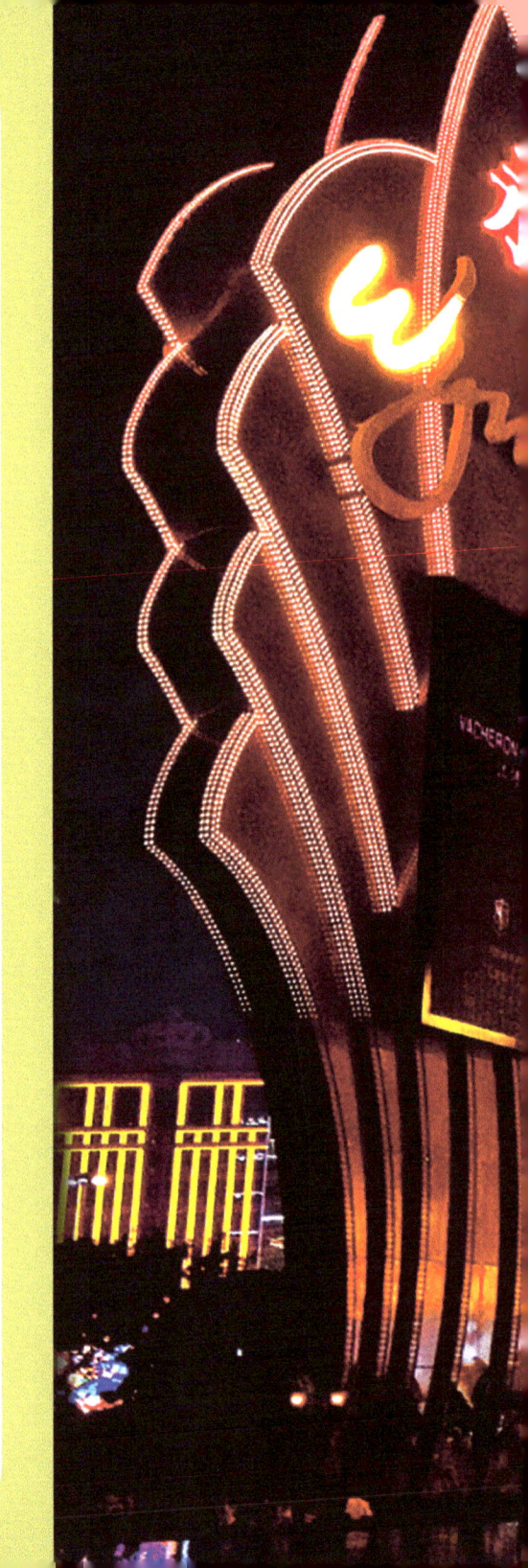

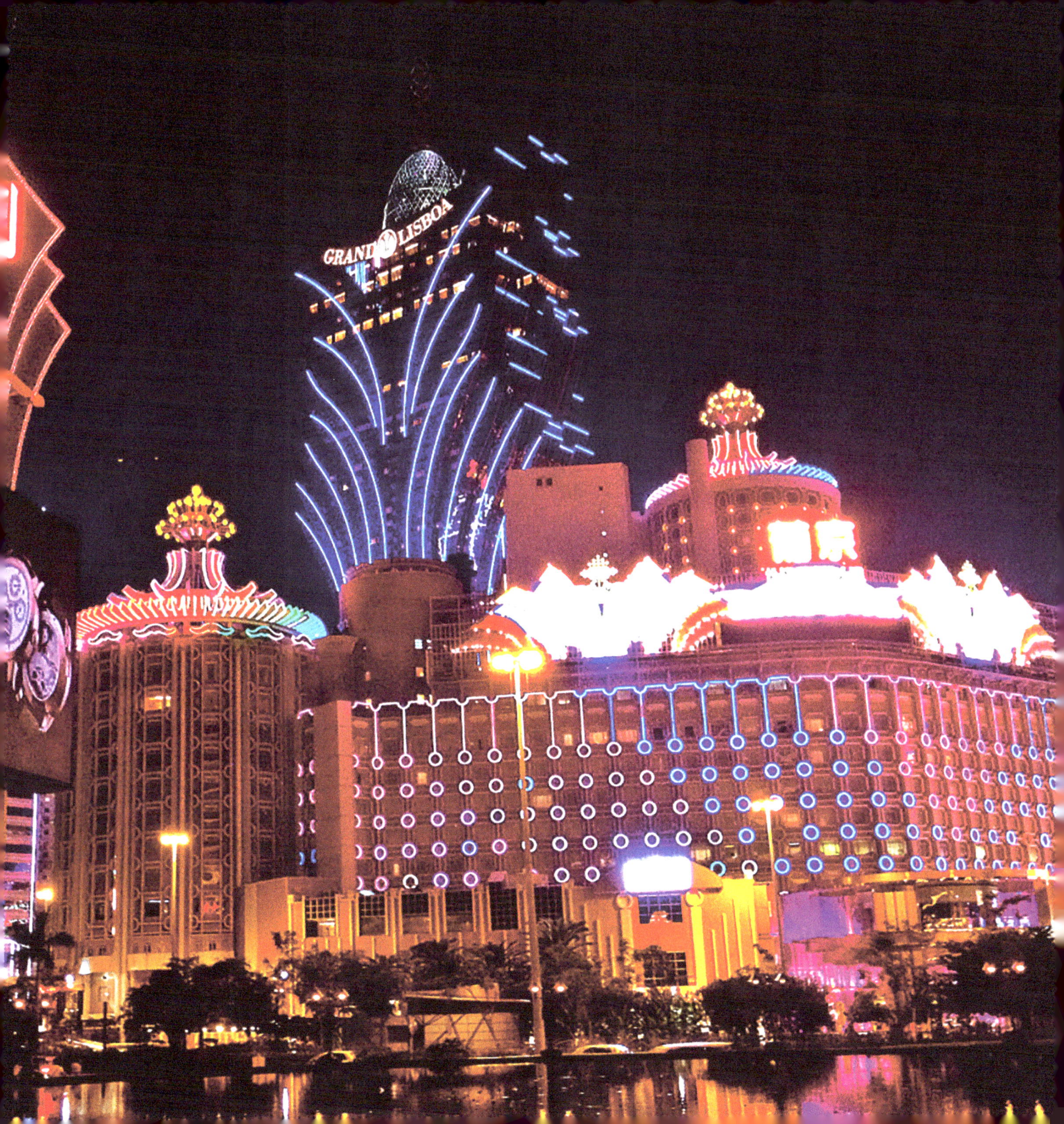
GRAND LISBOA

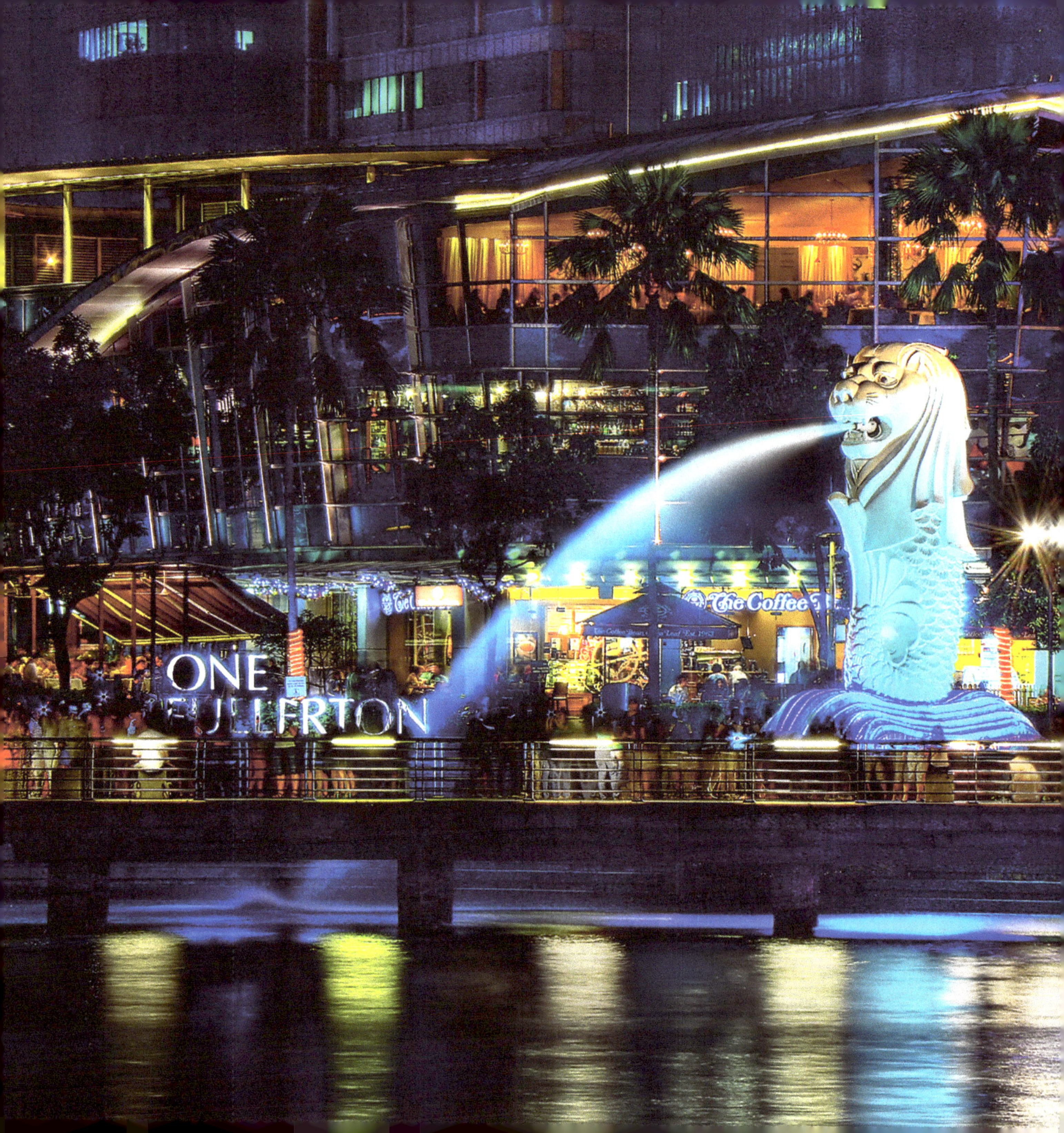
ONE
FULLERTON
The Coffee

SINGAPORE

Singapore is the home of the world's first night zoo, called the Night Safari. The Night Safari uses specially designed lighting that looks like moonlight. The animals in the zoo roam freely about in the rainforest and are separated by moats from the visitors.

AFGHANISTAN

The city of Herat in Afghanistan was most likely either the ancient Persian town of Artacoana or Aria established before 500 BC. The older section of the city is partly encircled by the ruins of massive walls of mud. Several monuments are still standing.

CENTRAL ASIA

KYRGYZSTAN

The country of Kyrgyzstan is located on the ancient trade route between China and the Mediterranean called the Silk Road.

UZBEKISTAN

The city of Tashkent in Uzbekistan has one of the most beautiful mass transit train stations in the world. It has ceilings and pillars made of marble, chandeliers, and engraved metal.

RUSSIA (ASIAN SECTION)

Most of the 143 million people in Russia live in the European part of the country. Only about 33 million people live in the Asian part of the country due to its freezing climate. Lake Baikal in the south of Siberia is the world's deepest lake. The Trans-Siberian Railway passes Baikal as it travels on its route between Moscow and the Sea of Japan.

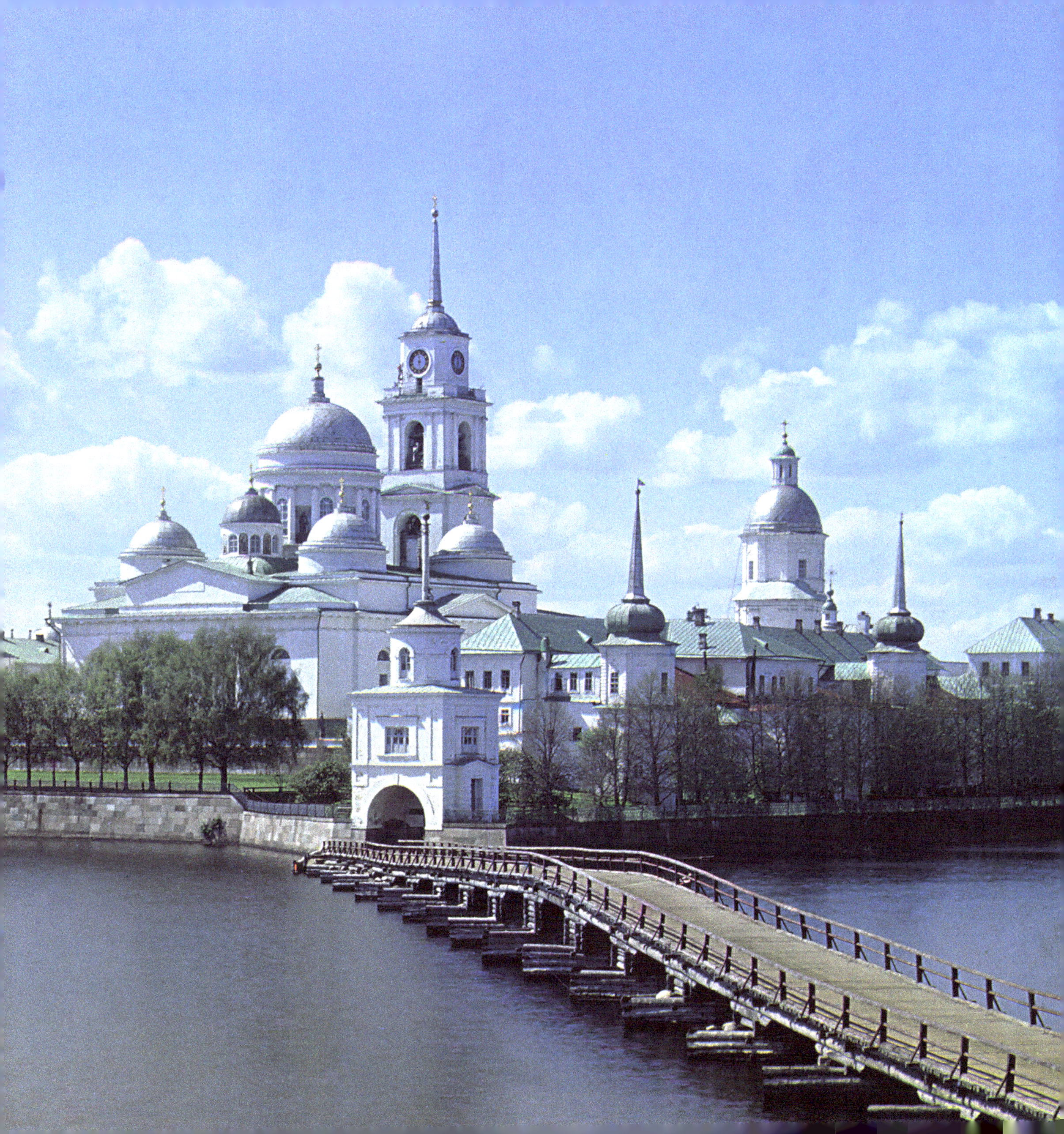

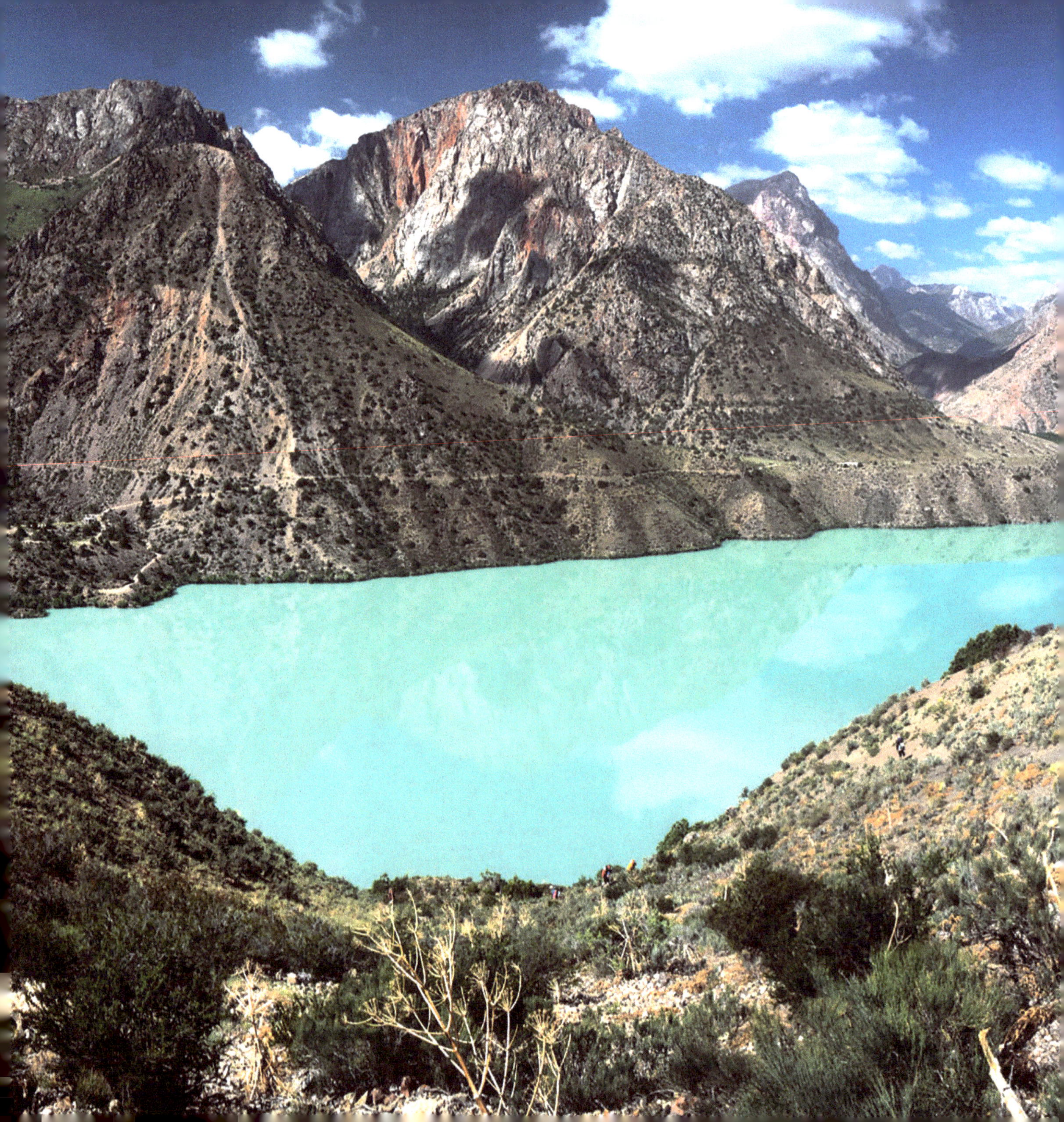

TAJIKISTAN

The country of Tajikistan borders Afghanistan, China, Kyrgyzstan, and Uzbekistan. It's known for its rugged mountains popular with hikers and climbers. Iskanderkulsky Nature Refuge, with its gorgeous, turquoise Iskanderkul lake surrounded by glaciers, is a well-known bird habitat.

CHINA

Considered one of the new Seven Wonders of the World, the Great Wall of China was built in the 7th Century Bc to protect China from invaders. The wall, which runs for over 4,000 miles, took hundreds of years to construct. It's the only manmade structure that can be seen from space.

EAST ASIA

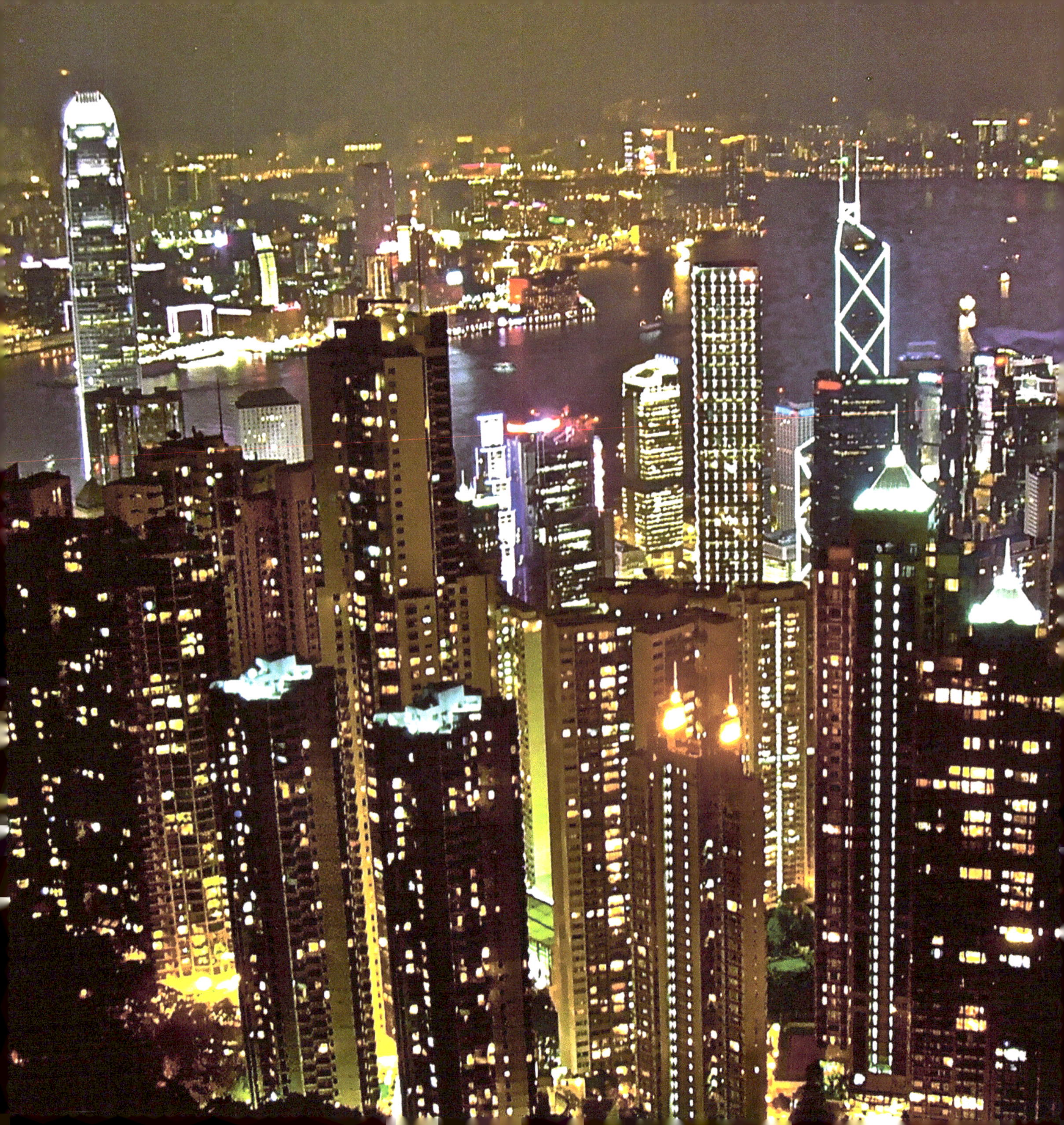

HONG KONG

Formerly a British colony, Hong Kong became a special administrative region of the People's Republic of China in 1984. As of 1997, it's operated under the principle of "one country, two systems," which means it's allowed to be independent. Hong Kong is famous for its skyline of skyscrapers and its gorgeous harbor.

JAPAN

Japan is an island nation off the east coast of China in the Pacific Ocean. The crowded capital of Tokyo is famous for its bright neon skyscrapers and pop culture. The city of Kyoto has beautiful Buddhist temples, peaceful Shinto shrines, and fragrant cherry blossoms during the spring season.

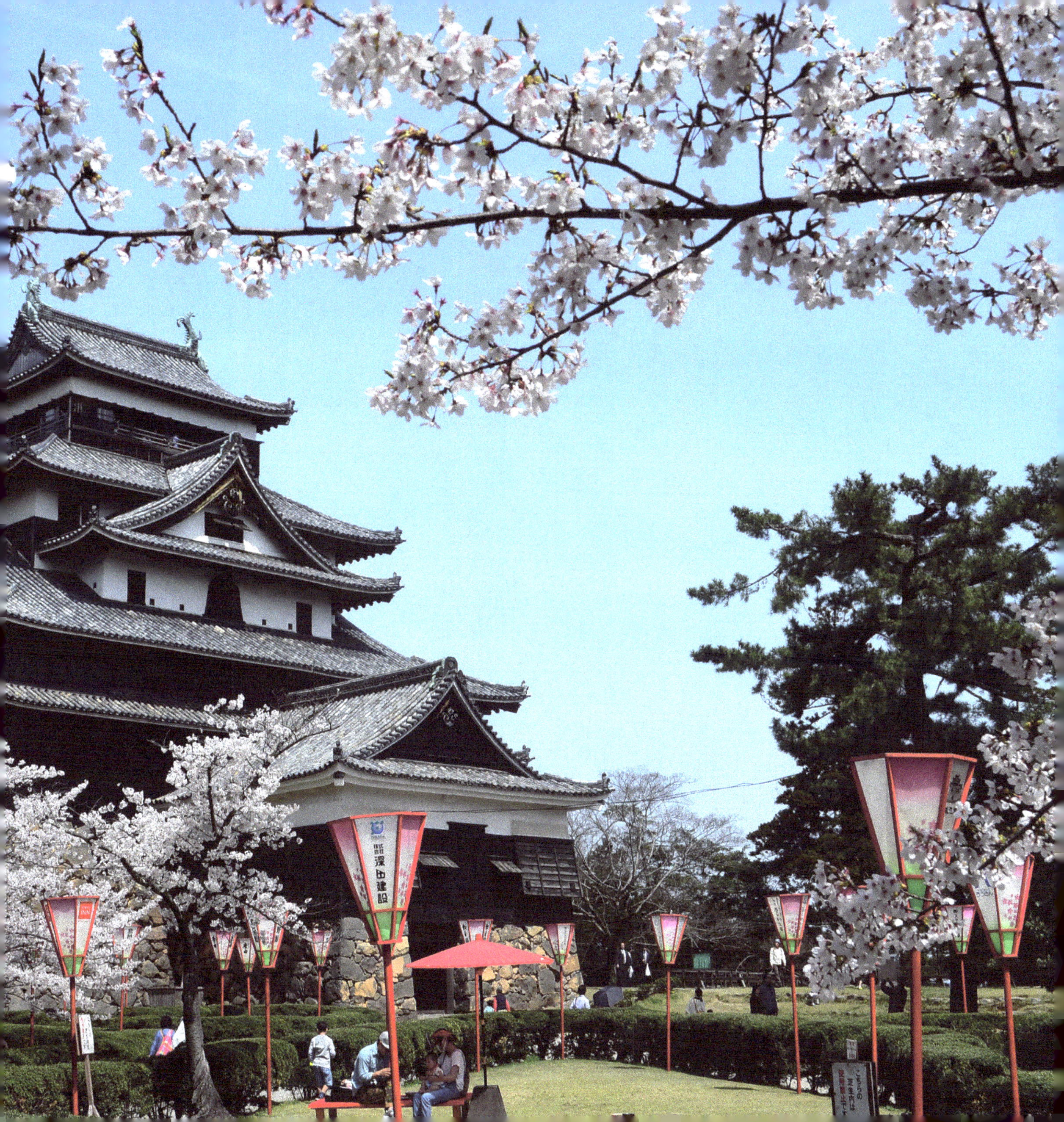
株式会社
深田建設

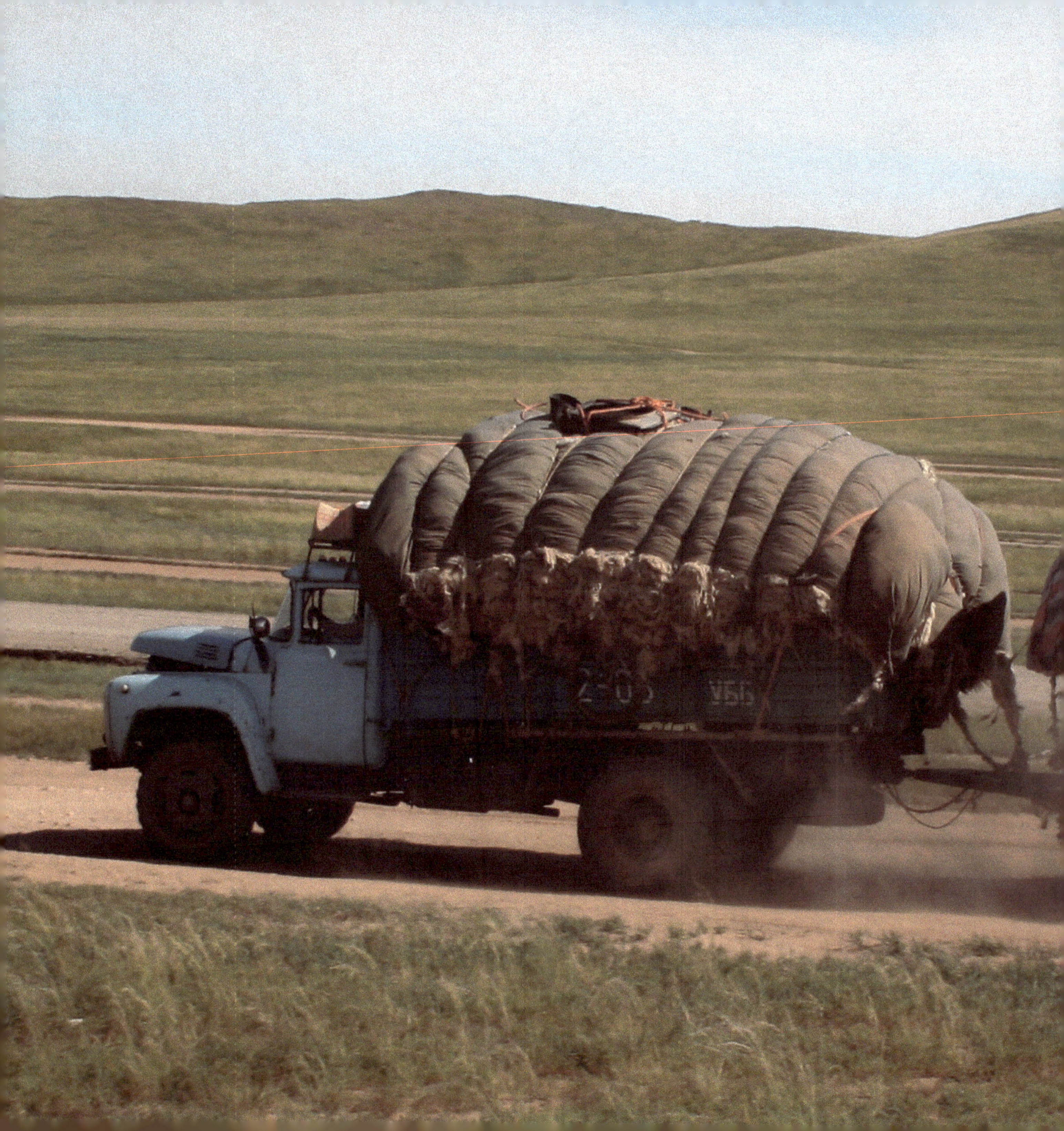

MONGOLIA

A landlocked nation, bordered by Russia to its north and China to its south, Mongolia is known for its large tracts of rugged land and its nomadic people. Its capital city, Ulaanbaatar, has the Genghis Khan Square, which was named after the founder of the Mongol Empire.

NORTH KOREA

In the 1950s, North Korea built a city called Kijŏng-dong. It was near the border of South Korea and meant to attract soldiers to cross the border and live in North Korea. The idea didn't work and the city is a "ghost city."

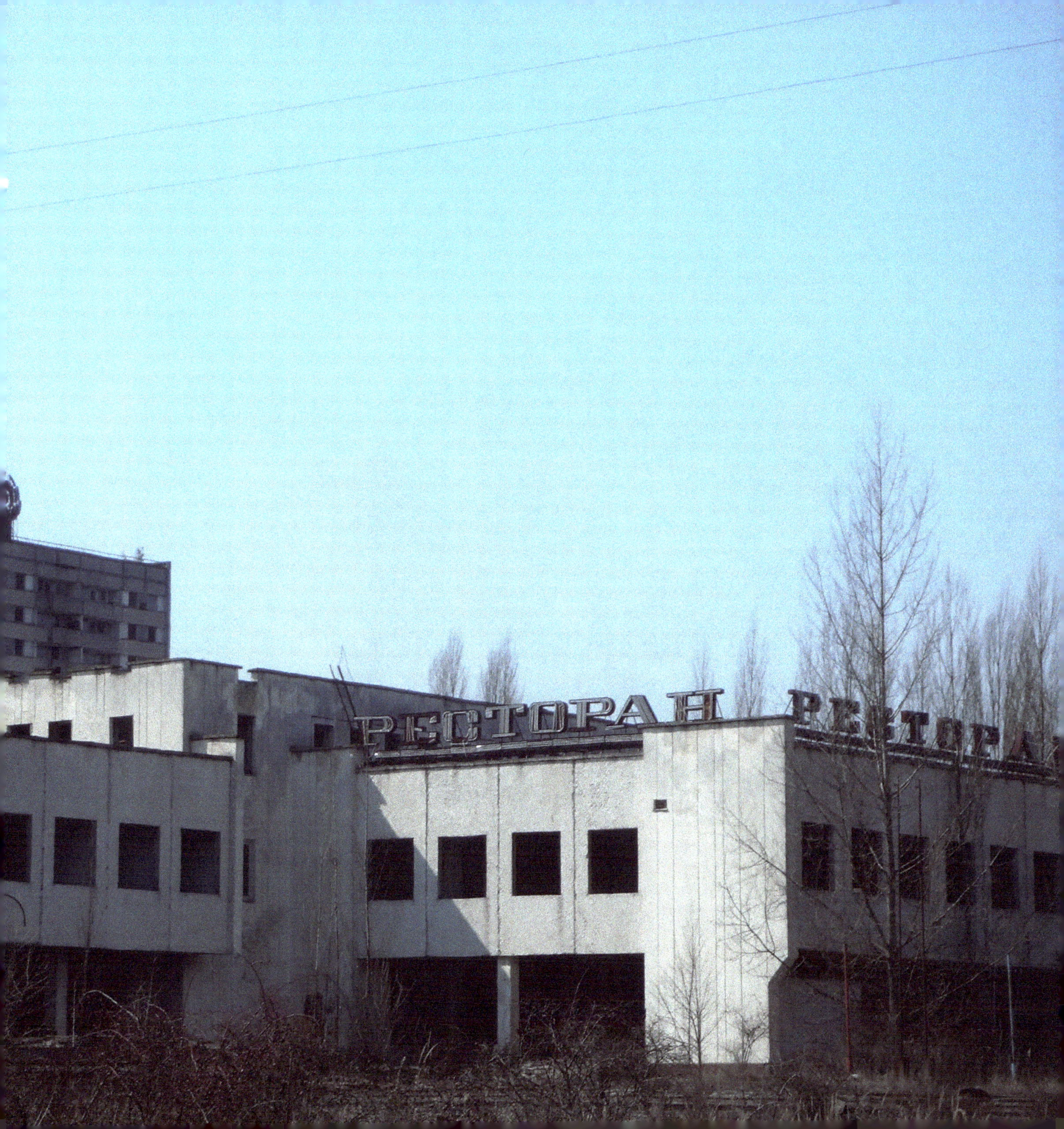
РЕСТОРАН

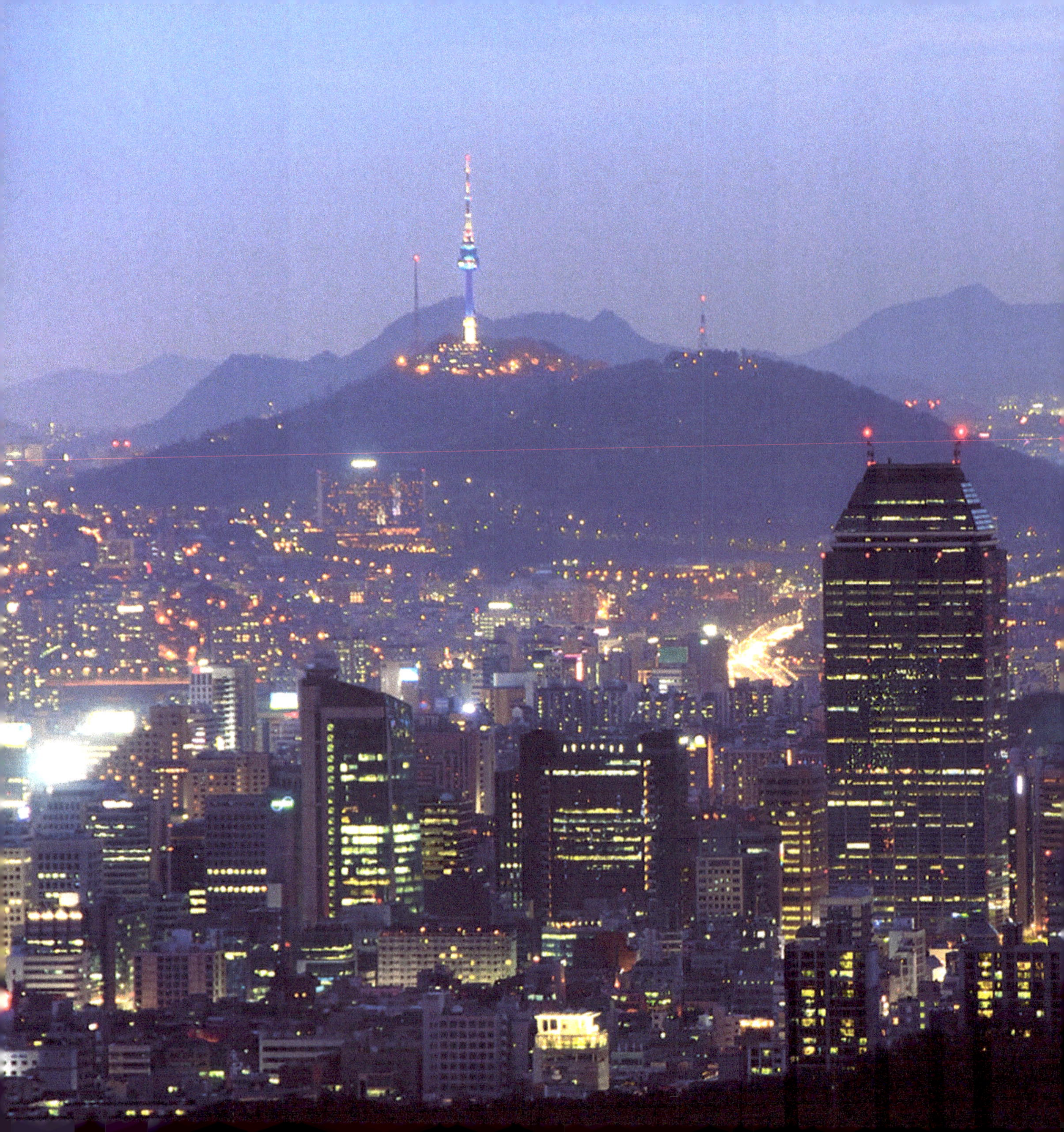

SOUTH KOREA

South Korea is located on the southern portion of the peninsula shared with North Korea. The border between the two countries has strong military forces on both sides. The city of Songdo in South Korea has been named the "World's Smartest City" because it was built with new technology advancements not available in most older cities.

TAIWAN

The country of China considers the island of Taiwan to be part of China, but Taiwan has a democratic government. It also has its own economy and currency. Its capital city of Taipei is known for Taipei 101, which is a 1,670 feet tall skyscraper shaped like a bamboo pagoda.

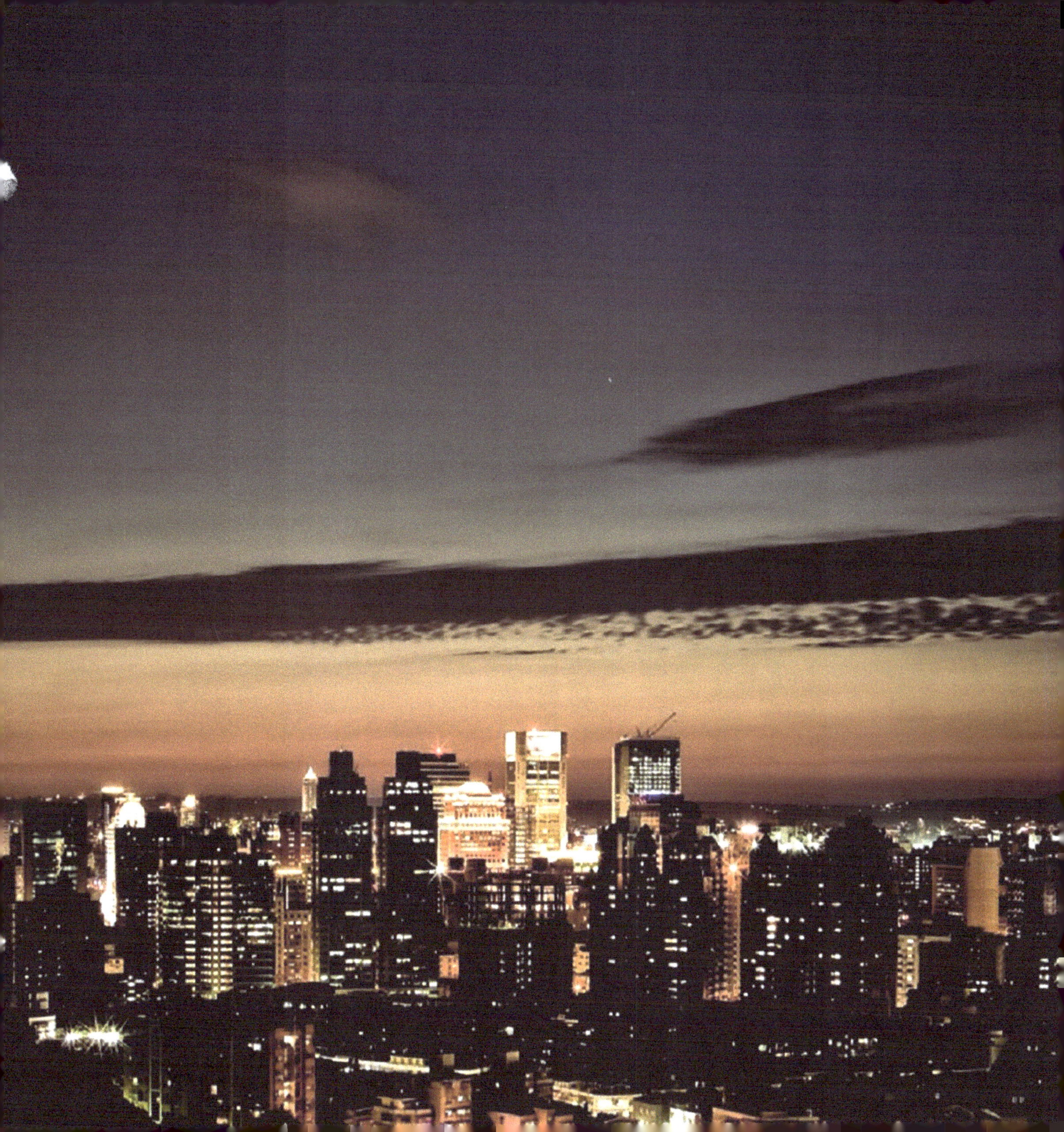

WEST ASIA

West Asia is the same as the Middle East. Turkey is the most populated country in West Asia. About 30% of the world's supply of oil comes from West Asia.

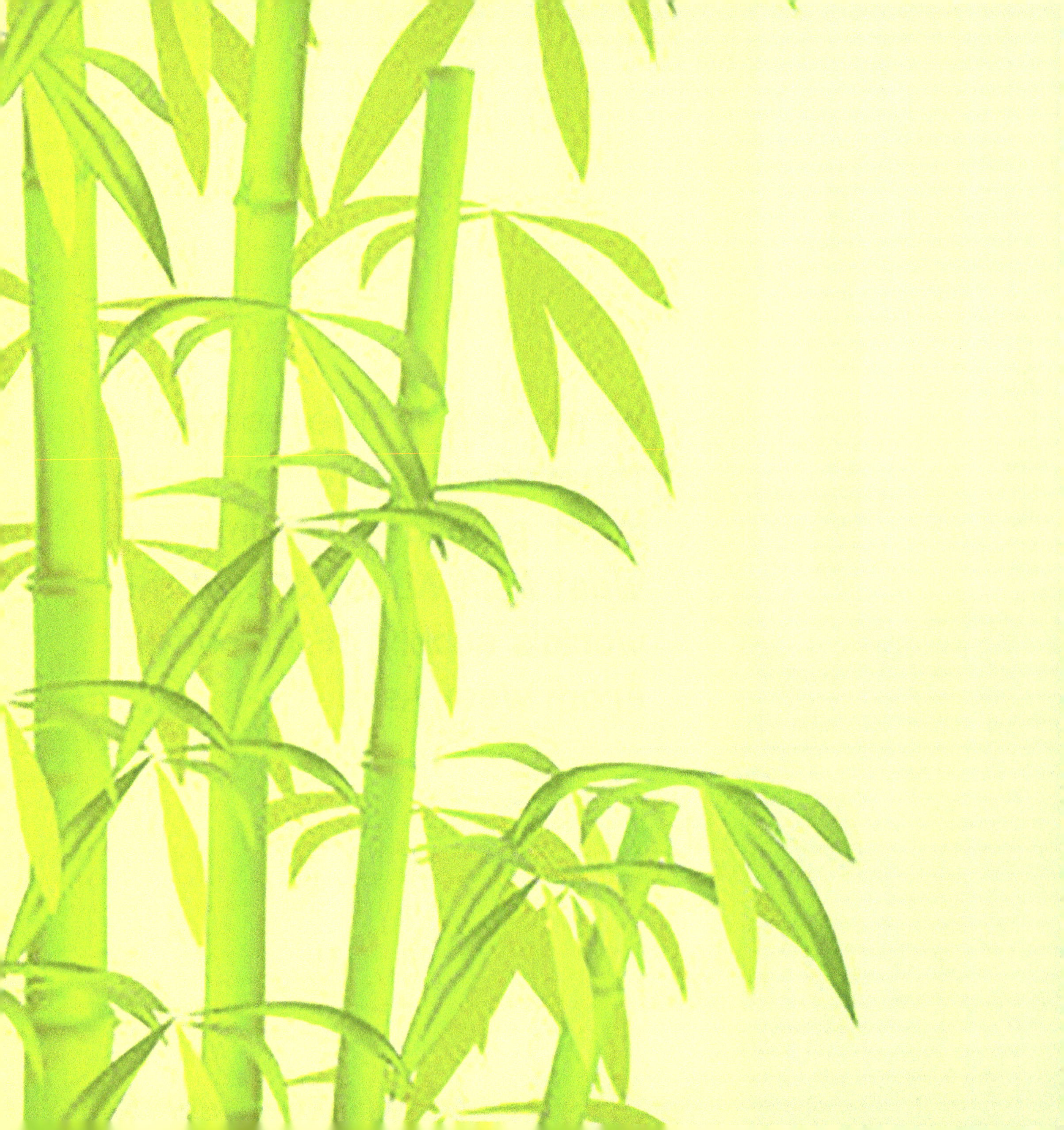

Awesome! Now you know more about the amazing continent of Asia. You can find more Geography and Culture books from Baby Professor by searching the website of your favorite book retailer.

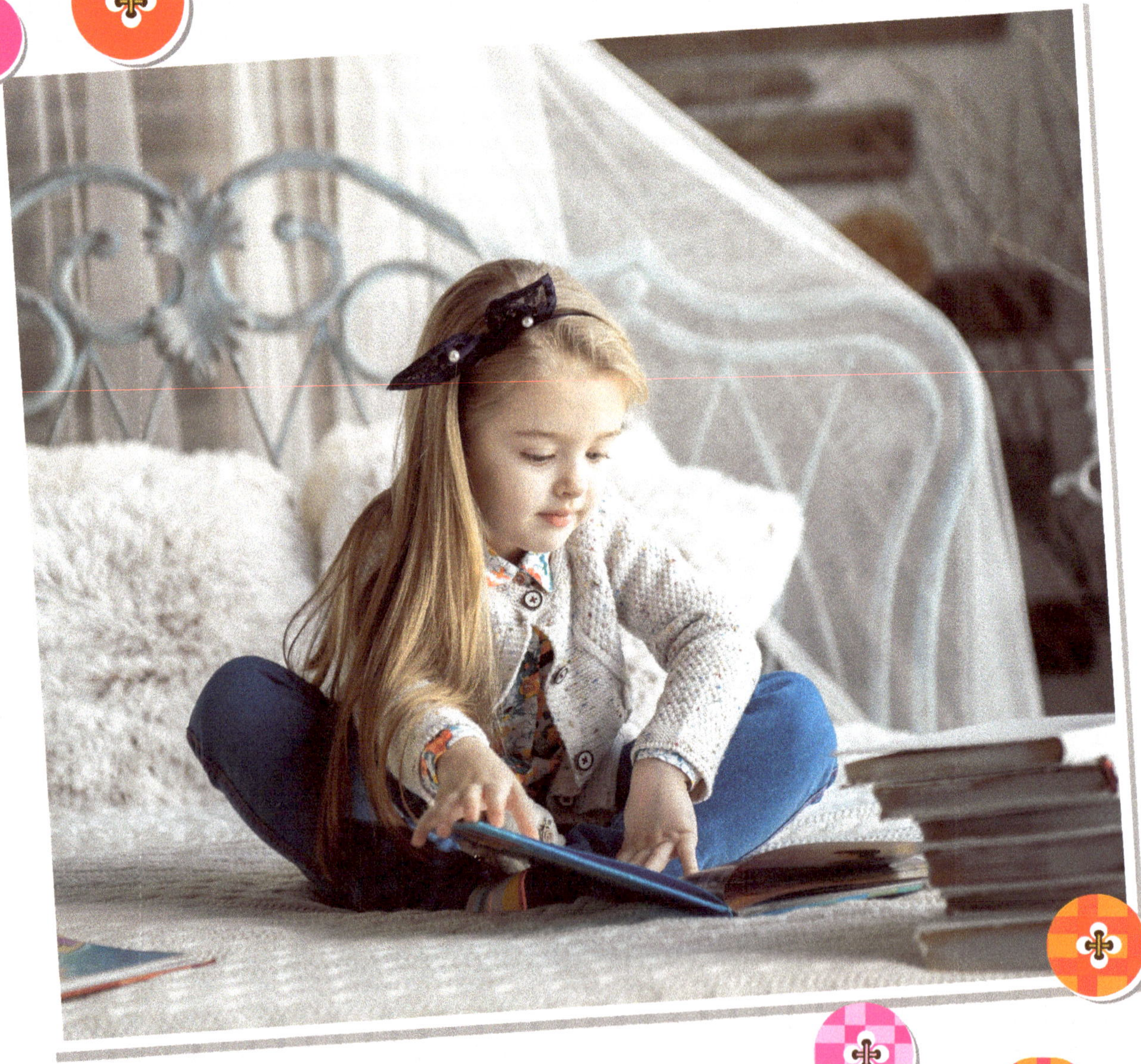

Visit

BABY PROFESSOR
EDUCATION KIDS

www.BabyProfessorBooks.com

to download Free Baby Professor eBooks and view our catalog of new and exciting Children's Books